You add Colour t, just by being

Lisa Scott

ROOTS

A Poetry Collection

Written by

Lisa Scott

© oakmoon. and. moss. poet.

Copyright © 2023 Lisa Scott. All rights reserved

No part of this publication may be reproduced, distributed, or transmitted in any form or by any means, including photocopying, recording, or other electronic or mechanical methods, without the prior written permission of the publisher, except in the case of brief quotations embodied in critical reviews and certain other non-commercial uses permitted by copyright law.

Cover illustration by Mark Forster

ISBN: **9798392887132**

DEDICATION

To my parents Lynne and David, for giving me my love of books, words and a childhood full of adventure. I am forever grateful for your constant love and support and for always believing in my dreams.

CONTENTS

Acknowledgments	1
Two Drops of Rain	3
Wax	5
Laughter	6
Drowning	7
Lost	9
Shelter	10
Roots	11
To My Young Self	13
Ladybird	15
Choice	16
Mother	17
Delicate	18
Warrior	19
Lungs	21
Free	22
Endless Gust	23
Beautiful Disaster	25

CONTENTS

Mona Lisa	26
The Swing	27
Tears	28
Autumn Wanderer	29
Wild Things	30
Dandelion	31
Wakeful Dream	33
Time	34
The Discovery Trail	35
Insecurity	37
The Voice Inside	38
Walking Shoes	39
People Watching	41
Silver Dreams	42
Flow	43
Aura	45
Heart in the wood	46

CONTENTS

Sea glass	47
Pheonix Sky	49
Forward	50
Equilibrium	51
World On Hold	53
Destiny	54
Clear Waters	55
The Edge	57
Purpose	58
Dreamstress	59
Ghost	61
Paint and Poetry	62
Written in Blue	63
Home	65
Skin	66
Magic	67
Unrequited	69

CONTENTS

Unreachable Winds	70
Annabel's Lullaby	71
Never Our Time	73
Dreamscape	74
Love to Dream	75
Longing	76
I Needed You	77
Your Silence	78
Earths Embrace	79
Teach Me How To Dance	80
Kiss Me	81
Bittersweet	82
Water and Fire	83
Jealousy	85
Springs Romance	86
Stung	87
Waves	89

CONTENTS

Burn the Boats	90
Letting Go	91
Soul of Everything	93
Sweet Nothings	94
Definition of Love	95
Lost in a Moment	97
My Last Letter	98
Stars	99
You Are Poetry	101
George	103
Beautiful Life	10

ACKNOWLEDGMENTS

Since being a small child I have suffered from anxiety, it is overwhelming and sometimes lonely. I've felt a real low and lack of self-confidence, I've felt crushed and unable to breathe, worry consuming every part of my body. I've learnt to cope through my writing, I find moments of joy in the nature around me, the sounds of the sea or the wind in the trees. Little by little, day by day, learning to breathe in the solitude of my mind.

I am lucky enough to know and have known the best family and friends I could wish for, who have given me advise, support and an ear when I have needed it. For that I am truly grateful.

To George, without you I don't know where I would be, you gave me a reason to get out of bed every day, love me unconditionally and without judgement. We have been on so many adventures together, you are my whole world. Your pawprints will forever be in my heart.

TWO DROPS OF RAIN

The soft murmur of the wind rattled against the windows. Nestled under the covers, a young girl shone a torch on her dreams. Bending the binding of countless stories in the glory of her imagination. The pitter patter of raindrops like galloping horses ran with the beat of her fragile heart, racing amongst the pages. Her inner soul a wanderer, well-travelled among new worlds. Unravelling her destiny, she skipped through the minds of her idols, lived in their day dreams. Picking at the seams of reality as anxieties of the new day tortured her worried soul. Why couldn't she jump through ink filled fantasies? Run bare foot through acre wood? Befriend the giants of her fears? Splash in the puddles of her tears? She danced on a rhythm of words. She was a girl filled with nonsense. Present but always absent. Escaping was all she ever wished, for would they miss the girl that didn't want to exist?
Moonlight shone from the window and stars dazzled like diamonds through watery orbs. Sitting for a moment lost in thought. Gripping a pen that eased her pain, she wrote a poem for the first time….there was two drops of rain.

ROOTS

WAX

The hue of the midnight sky
Flickers in the twilight
Memories a white clouded haze
An airborne quilt for the senses
A warm comfort as you dance through my mind
The aroma of melted wax
That once was cold and confined
Now surpassed into a river of soothing red
Molten memories splashed up the walls
Abstract smiles and words unsaid
Scraping the rainbows off forbidden canvas
Saved from the blackened bruises that awaited us
Dripping colour turning dark blue to green
Awakened an ocean of thought
Lessons given from you to me
Life burned through, innocence lost
Forever a flame burning in my heart
Your candle went out but never forgot
Lives on with the scent of this crayon box

LAUGHTER

The sweet notes filled my ears. Dancing through every hair on my neck. A choreography of magic that traced the braille of happiness on my skin. Vibrating the love notes of my soul that echoed a symphony in return. A silence now shattered that burns anger into ashes, as each breath passes through the ache in my ribs and drums with the heart beat of the earth. A ringing chime that stands still the bells of time, brightening up this world of mine.

DROWNING

Under the shallow waters, crisp currents grasp small fingers, luring a daughter to the depths. A sirens song clung to ears and the sweet ocean hum melted away fear. The surface a kaleidoscope of dancing sunlight illuminating the darkness. This silent underworld cushioned her body as light as a cloud, filling her lungs with the heaviest of doubt. A dreamer of mermaids as dreams clung to disappointment. A little girl that could not swim, now tangled in a torture of waves. Bathed with the hope of making them see, this girl was more than she could be.
Her heart finds a slow rhythm as two hands pull her towards loving arms. He will always keep her safe from harm. Coughing up the anxieties that kept her choked. A lump of silence that remains stuck in her throat. Still drowning unable to place her feet. Still treading the waters of life's defeats. With dreams the sails to solid ground, to one day stand and make them proud.

ROOTS

LOST

There must be a place where the imaginary things go
Once forgotten from the creators mind
Unknown, unseen, impossible to find
Lost in the oubliette as dark memories are left to forget with time
A closeted skeleton of a world once mine
A figment of a friend, banished from the human eye
But I saw you and they didn't understand why
My forearms bloody raw from the grip of frustration
You stood by me in the shadows of my imagination
Even brave hearts can drown in breathless waves
But your light made rainbows through the graves of yesterday
With each year I aged I watched you fade
And my life has slowly turned back to grey.

SHELTER

I sometimes visit my childhood home
Sit under the old chestnut tree
Its back worn with scars of little feet that climbed its sturdy branches
Claiming its fruit of knowledge
It knows me better than anyone
I've carved my secrets into its soul
It has watched me fall and rise and fall and grow
And like its leaves that decay and rot to the earth
It has watched me grow into a woman from a girl
My tears have soaked into its roots, quenching my pains
And here you stand, remaining where you are
As your limbs wrap around my heart
Pointing to the stars
You hold so much history, felt loss like no one has
A sadness that brings winters wilt
Knowing that one day I too shall pass
But you will hold the whisper of my thoughts in your leaves
And my smile will dance with blossom in the breeze
I will bring from the heavens, the April rains
So you will shelter the next generation
As the seasons begin to change.

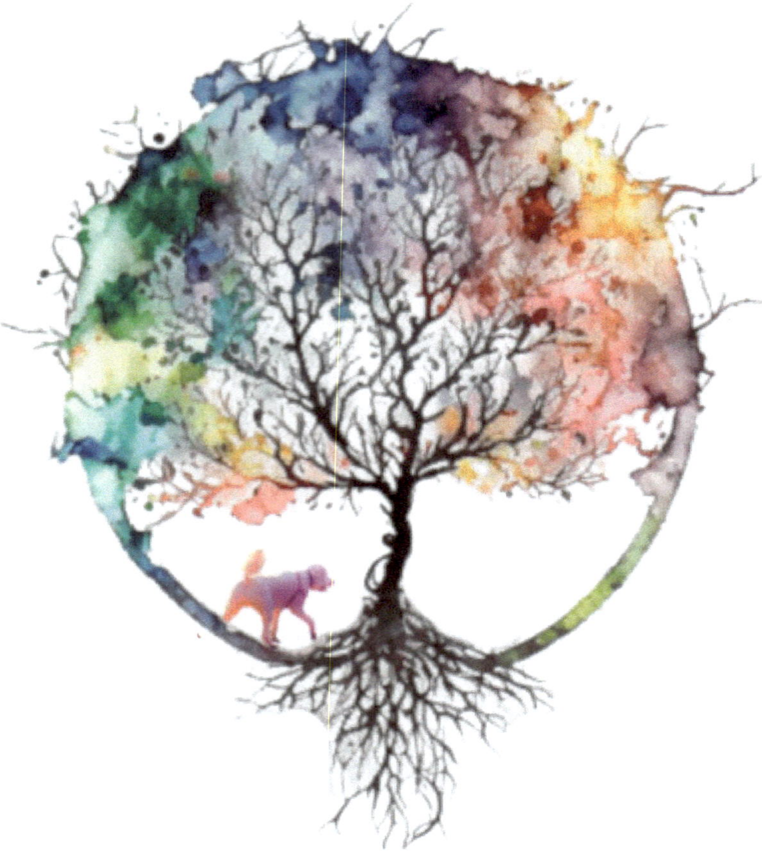

ROOTS

I love my family… I do.
But I'm just one branch on this sturdy family tree. One branch waiting to blossom, looking at the earth through the rain. Weathered by storms and growing lichens to patch my wounds, filling the voids, padding out the emptiness. Arms constantly reaching towards the clouds. Praying for winds that will carry me and take me on a new path, journeying to unknown places. Float along the Yangtze river. Embed into the nest of eagles. I'm just waiting, waiting to forsake and be free. To be cut from this life and thrown for the dogs, for even that would be more exhilarating. Burn me as firewood, let me smolder and my smoke rise high, free flowing into the universe. Or turn me into pulp, into paper. Let me feel the depth of peoples words, let me live their stories. Let me experience love. Let my roots become entwined with another, pollinating with the sweetness of our nectar, creating new seeds of life.
Every year I grow the leaves of dreams, they show the maps of the places I will never visit, and I watch as the decay of winter takes them. Watching as they wither and wilt. Their beautiful colours fading into the rotting earth. And every year I grow more hope, more dreams, waiting for them to bloom but it never happens. I'm a prisoner to this tree, forever bound to its foundations.
Waiting for that day there is finally a swing of escape. Tied around my neck. Tightening with each pull as children play.
Choking as I feared I would
Letting go of this sheltered life
                      Before I
                            Finally
                                  Break

TO MY YOUNG SELF

To you, my young self
To fragile and shy
To afraid to ask for help
With no confidence to try
You will grow to be strong
People around you to confide
So don't be ashamed
Bring out the self that you hide

To you, my young self
It's ok to feel lost
You will become a wanderer
And through nature
Find yourself on paths crossed

Don't cry over things you couldn't control
Anxiety will still consume you
But you will never be alone
Don't give up on your dreaming
Keep your imagination alive
Let words fall to paper
Watch your creativity thrive

To you, my young self
A broken heart will never mend
But you will still love with its pieces
Your love ones and friends
Trust won't come easy
You will have scars from being burnt
But you will grow from the ashes
And the lessons you've learnt

Love yourself and remember
To never compare
Live life at your own pace
There's no race to get there
You may never get married
Or have children of your own
But you will stand proud of where you are
And how much you have grown
From a girl to a woman
Through your trauma and pain
Leaving the past in the past
Accepting you will never be the same

Change is a good thing
And with it you will grow
Take chances and move
Follow your heart where it goes
See the world through your eyes
The child that you are
Keep your innocence and have fun
Always look up at the stars

To you, my young self
Realise time comes without cost
It's worth more than money
Memories will never be forgot
Run through the forests
Kiss under oaks
Let laughter echo through the hills
In the places you walk

You have a long way to go
But your smile still remains true
You are beautiful and never forget
There's only one authentic you.

LADYBIRD

We had fairies at the bottom of our garden once, my mother sent me to find them. I would hear them giggle and hide amongst the flowers as I blew bubbles for hours in the sunlight. They would rest upon the grass and I would chase the magic until at last they popped.
The world has a better view upside down, hands touching grass, feet towards the blue, cartwheeling in a day dream.
To lie in a botanical wilderness, creating shapes out of clouds and singing aloud the nursery rhymes of generations past. Making daisy chains that won't last as they wilt in the shade of the afternoon.
Sweet lemonade and buttercup kisses on my chin, oh to be a child again. In my wonderland, my fortress, on my swing flying high, covered in ladybirds as I count the spots on their wings.
Collecting all things bright and beautiful in a jar, blowing dandelion moon wishes towards the stars.
Time fades the days without request, I now walk barefoot where my childhood came to rest. Feeling the blades beneath my toes, following the memories as they flow from my mind.
I lie on the ground listening for the sound of fluttering wings, closing my eyes to everything around me. I slip into a sea of tranquillity, back to a time only a child's eyes could see, and the earth slows with the calm, as a ladybird comes to rest on my arm…

CHOICE

You don't understand, you don't have kids

But maybe I wanted them but now it's too late
Maybe that choice was taken away with age
Maybe this loss is the pain I contain

You don't understand, you don't have kids

But maybe I have other things in my care
Things that wouldn't survive without me there
Little heartbeats at my feet, leaving footprints on the floor
I have tails instead of little hands greeting me at the door

You don't understand, you don't have kids

Maybe I'm playful, content and free
Maybe I don't need children to see
I climb mountains, hills and beautiful trees
But my me time must be so selfish of me

You don't understand, you don't have kids

I'm tired of not being accepted as a friend
Because I didn't take the path that life intends
Not being included in the mothers circle
Because what would I know about being maternal

YOU don't understand, the freedom of choice

Just like the freedom you were given when you expressed your voice
It's hard enough being a woman
We are not all the same
Choosing not to have children shouldn't come with the shame.

MOTHER

I miss her
I miss how she shakes me from my dreams as reality bites
Or how we sit for hours over coffee
As we set the world to right
I miss the details of her face that resembles mine
A life time of laughter and tears
Emotions and fears
Represented by one line….a wrinkle
And as my own fire of strength starts to die
I miss how she would poke at the embers
To keep my inner flame of dreams alive
I miss her caring and forgiving nature
That loves me to my very core
The bravest woman I know, through the pain you endure
You've danced with my demons
Pardoned a lifetime of sins
You protect me from harm
Under hidden angel wings.

DELICATE

She is a wild flower
She is the sun's energy
The rain's power
She is delicate
Roots entwined with the earth's soul
She is the blush flare of her own light
Yellow heart a radiant glow
She is the linger of spring's sanctuary
She grows through the thorn's clutch
Her skin bejewelled by sunrise
Through the winds that keep her hushed
Beautiful petals chained in perfect floral knots
Whispered weeds to answer question
To love her or love her not
Swirl of dew dropped rainbows
Through the eyes of the beguiled
Her seeded strength, the wings of angels
Untamed as the summer sky
She grows in hearts that dream
The moonlight bends to watch her rise
Admire her from a distance
But love her in all her wild.

WARRIOR

I am a warrior with many voices
I sit on a mirrored throne reflecting so many versions of myself
Crying for the help of the stars that split my path
A map for a dreamer with an over filled head
A line between living and the walking dead
I lie in my bed of words that rhyme with no reason
Spilling my ink with the rain of the seasons
I swim in this deep puddle of doubts
Waiting for warmth and a few days of drought
To rest this head, this worried soul
The more I take, the less comfort I know
Grasping life like a fist full of water
Quenching temporary thirsts, always the daughter
Walking the cobbled stone pathways of memory lane
Striving to climb mountains and deep terrain
Electrolytes of my brain that put out fires
A heart that beats with the deepest desires
To see my reflection in the rivers of truth
A sadness that makes my green eyes blue
But I stand with my blessings that I recount
And start to love from the inside out.

ROOTS

LUNGS

Polluted air of smoke filled thoughts
Decomposing soul born of the earth
The truth in which she breathes
Choking on fear, dust and dirt
Circulated icy air, wheezing in the breeze
Spiralling airstreams of hope
Whistled though the holes of insecurities
Hurtful words will never iron out
Crumpled creases of the pain
Discarded like a piece of trash
Soaked in puddles of last nights rain
Drowning in this ribcage
Waves of anxiety make me choke
Clawing at my tongue
To stop the hate that you provoke
Tattooed are the memories
On the walls of paper thin dreams
Tearing through the storm filled clouds
And the whispers of the trees
A cyclone of paranoia
The heart a distant beat
An echo of silence brings a calm
Learning once again to breathe.

FREE

When I am alone, I become invisible
Sitting in the long grass as daisies push through the earth to greet my soul
My body leaves this shell and drifts along the rivers currents
Swirls of colour fill my mind
I find peace as I open my ears to the sounds
A blackbird sings from a distant canopy
A woodpecker knocks frantically above
When I am alone, I become her daughter
Dancing on her breeze along the forest floor
Buds burst open and seize the first sunlight of spring
The bees and butterflies alive with their scent
I feel the April rain trickle down my skin
The hairs on my neck stand to attention
As the thunder rolls with my heartbeat
When I am alone, I dance in my silence
The foxes chase my shadow under the moon
The loon calls across the pond
A magical stardust that dazzles the surface
The heron stands to attention, waiting in the white noise
Waiting for a dream to drift along the riverbed
The ether of love squeezing through the voids of every pebble
When I am alone, I am blind but I see
The new world behind my eyes
I feel as light as a feather and as soft as a cloud
Only grounded by the earth between my toes
My chakras align in unison within me
Energy seeping through the pores of my skin
A calling to the universe and all she sees
For when I am alone
I am free.

ENDLESS GUST

A leaf drifts on an endless gust
Lost in a sea of Autumn's rush
A sound of rustle as it swirls the floor
Vibrant but still invisible to the core

Anxiously waiting to rest on the ground
To be crunched under foot and make a sound
Seeking the rains and winter's bite
But the frost nestles at the core in the shiver of night

A beating heart under beating sun
Golden breeze that has begun
Teased and tormented as trees undress
Beauty in tattered distress

A leaf that drifts on an endless gust
Lost in a fiery crowd of nature's dust
Storm after storm
Caged in a swirl of society
Storm after storm
Contant anxiety.

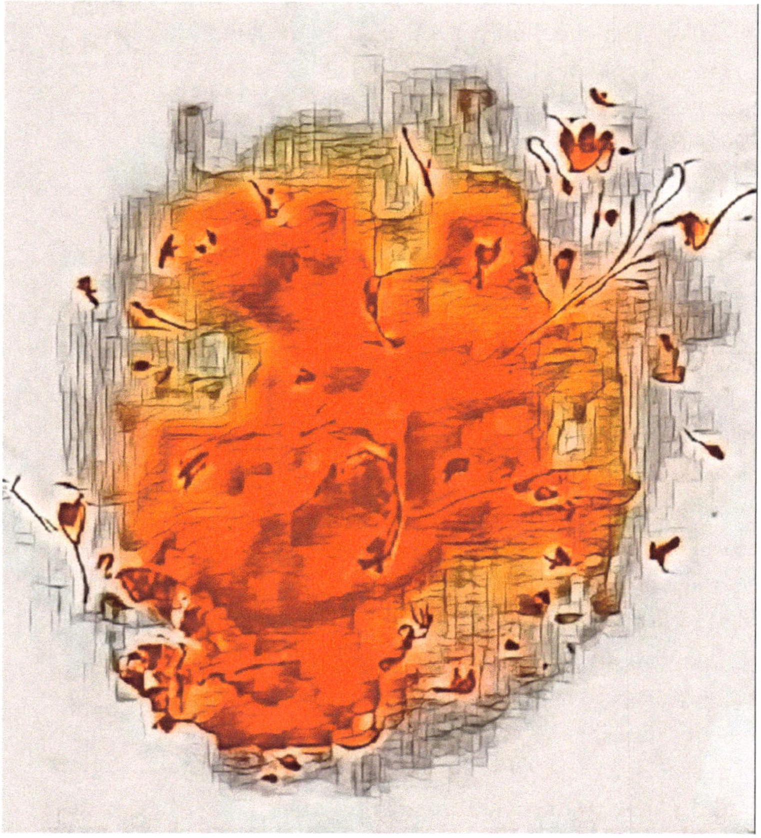

BEAUTIFUL DISASTER

How can anyone know me if I don't know myself
Like shards of a fragmented mirror reflected by the sun
My souls shines deeply but partially
On selected eyes that look upon
Everyone wants a piece
A reflection of themselves
But my sharp edges cut deep
And bleeds into dreams as they sleep
Nights that creep and swallow me whole
Do I sit in the shadows?
Or the light of the moon's beckoning call?
I live in a life of constant grey
Absorbing my day to day chaos
Emotionally charged but energy low
I carry my body and presence like an exclamation point
Or a question mark
For answers already written in my bones
But you don't know
You don't know about the vibrant flame of pain in my chest
My heart that beats and it beats
Under anxieties duress
I must confess, I'm a mess
I smile with the strength through my sorrow
Fighting the torment of dreams for a better tomorrow
They say I am beautiful, I bring joy through my laughter
But I am just a shard of the mirror you see
I am a beautiful disaster.

MONA LISA

Mona Lisa
The woman with the enigmatic smile
Lips coated with serene stardust
Blending with natures curves and lines
A portrait of pain
Camouflaged in silk and linen leaves
Like a mute she signs her own language
And you choose what to believe
A temptress, feeding you with her flirtatious flaws
A masterpiece
Hiding the truth of her human soul
Intangible existence, trapped in a frame
A smile anchored to her fate
Melancholy tones to her name
Sins crawling through her skull
As the brush strokes of colour fade
Nails scrape to escape the canvas
Her soul on display
Those that look upon her beauty
Will forever be moved
Da Vinci's lost secret
The Lady of the Louvre

THE SWING

A feeling of weightlessness, as I freefall with the breeze
Back and forth with my uncertainties
An oscillatory motion as the force of momentum pushes me higher
Into the clouds of my imagination
As gravity pulls on the procrastination of ever changing winds
To sway and swing on life's pendulum
A wave of endless choice
Knowing my finest hour is not in the past
Never a repeat of days, but how long will they last?
An echo of a lost childhood playground in my chest
Laugher whirling through unresisting space
Bobbing and weaving trying to reach a place on the ground
Is it just luck by chance where the swinging stops?
Or do the fates intervene where we decide to get off?
I move to and fro with the gentleness of the spring breeze
Whilst the icy grip of winter pulls me to grazed knees
Stuck in a space of the in-between worlds
A star that burns bright to reach the Earth
True energy concealed in words never rehearsed
As the pendulum swings in a mind creating verse
A momentum beat on a rhythmic flight
Easing back and forth against a back drop of still born air
And it's there in the centre of love and loss
The ink drops from my pen and I momentarily stop
Lost
In the grand cadence of poetry.

TEARS

The heart can over flow sometimes
Gravity shifting my core like an earthquake
Emotions buried in the bones
Now rising to the surface
Through the eyes is where the clouds break
Cornered winter puddles surrounded by grief
Condensing the soul underneath
And droplets that words cannot speak
Falling to a salty freedom
Down ageing skin
I wish I could turn them off like a tap
Hide the weakness within
But I cannot stop the flood
The power of a waterfall catching the light
Will surely stop myself from diving
And drowning myself inside.

AUTUMN WANDERER

I take it all in
Every cloud in the dark Autumn sky
Every red leaf as it whips my cheek in the wind
I breathe the cold air through my lungs
And listen to the rain as it hits the puddles around me
And in the trees, crisp leaves on branches clung
Conkers in their spikey shells
A sign that winter has begun

I wrap up warm and walk with pace
I feel a sense of connection
To this wild world I face
Mother nature herself keeps pushing me yonder
Revealing her secrets of beauty
In the places I wander.

WILD THINGS

In my heart is where the wild things grow

Deep red rivers of love
That flow to the roar of the ocean
Swimming figures of the imagination
Luring in the depths, fighting for the light of the stars

In my heart is where the wild things grow

Butterfly wings through blossomed oak
A hurricane among the clouds
Red rains that stain the rainbows
Screaming with the flying larks

In my heart is where the wild things grow

A murmur of hope on a whispered breeze
Dancing with the woodpeckers beat
As snails trail the scars of tomorrow's worries
Sheltered under leaves as thunder starts

In my heart is where the wild things grow

An acorn that shoots arms to the sky
Dreams that catch light of the burning sun
A calmness that lifts and drifts to new days
A beat that turns into a melody and slows....

In my heart is where the wild things grow.

DANDELION

I live in a sea of emerald green wands
I flow with the waves of the breeze
I'm wild, I'm free, I have purpose
But to you I am only a weed…..

I am the sun by day in a warming yellow haze
I dance with the choreography of the bees
I'm strong, resilient, I'm not worthless
But to you I am only a weed….

By night I am the moon, my petals the stars
Fairytale wands and childhood dreams
I'm infinite, I am eternal, I resurface
But to you I am only a weed…..

My scattered soul was born to soar
This botanical world was mine to seize
I fly, I'm a seed, I'm earthless
But to you I am only a weed…...

I am the bounty of diversity, beauty in a form
No notion of place but I'm always at home
I grow in the pavements, the woods, under trees
I am a miracle in a world striving to succeed

But to you I am only a weed.

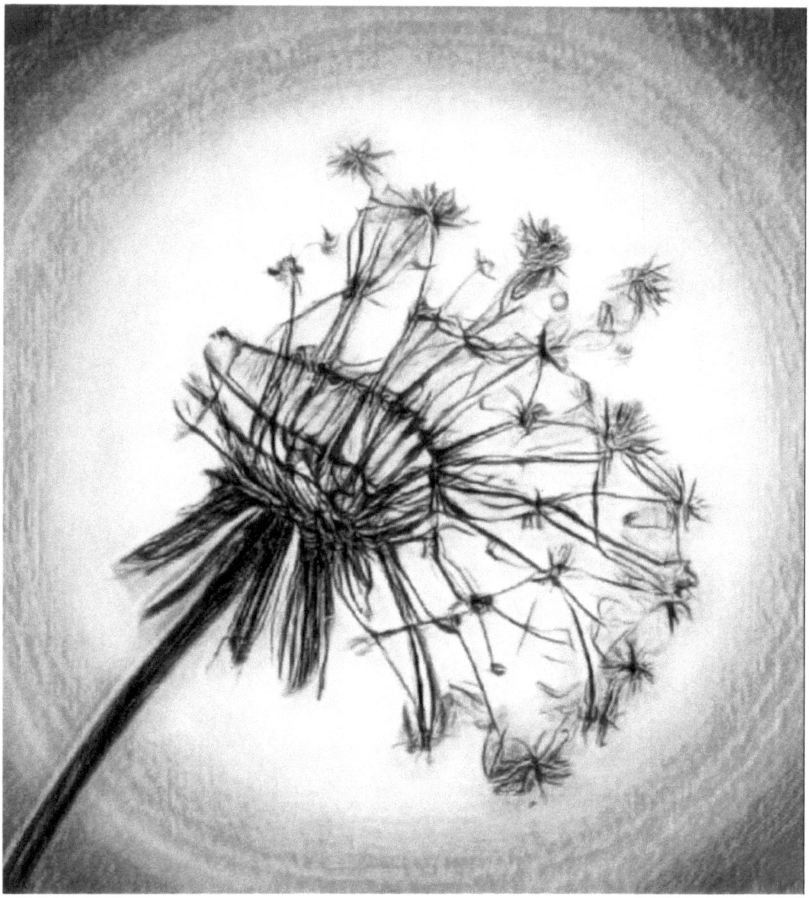

WAKEFUL DREAM

Anticipation warms my skin
As I take a step towards the mountain
Following the roar of the waterfall
And the pull of its power
I climb her steps, one by one
Breathe….
The sunlight teases through the canopies
Dancing on the water's surface like poetry
And I climb with the tranquillity
Inhaling the earth's scent
I climb her steps, one by one
Breathe….
Each exhale of my lungs
I turn and face the sun
A buzzard calls from above
And I'm surrounded by snow topped peaks
Lost in a moment
The crown of the world at my soles
And I hold the minutes, one by one
Breathe….
Taking in the artistic horizon
A world no one will ever see
Until you climb the heart of nature
Your sight will never look upon
A sense of a wakeful dream.

TIME

Time.
It surrounds me and suffocates me
A ticking brain but a broken clock
Hands that try to mend
A heart that never stops
A wounded beat, slightly out of sync with the world
Now a woman that holds the ghost of the girl
A mother to my old soul, singing memory lullabies
Each day fading into the hymn of her goodbyes
Time
It flows with the rivers, through the banks of crows feet
Seeping and quenching the thirst of hungry lips
Sugar and salt, the bitter, the sweet
Unable to turn back
Never now, always soon
As wings hatch from spring's cocoon
Dancing with the flowers in momentary bloom
Time
Grasping the sand grains that waterfall through my fingers
As each turn of the hourglass flows to build new mountains
My inner soul, the fountain of youth
Climbing to find her purpose and truth
Standing in midlife's fire of fate
To wait, to wander
But never too late.

THE DISCOVERY TRAIL

My soul embarks to light the dark
As the wind pried with stiff fingers
Pulling roots to the surface, on a path to accept my past and purpose
Words touched my lips like the morning dew
As pools of poems swirl in the centre of flowers that bow to a new day in the sunlight
My creative spirit feeds off the nectar and takes flight, carried with the sails of clouds
As my fingers swirl the ether between canopies untouched
An echo of a child's laughter as my inner self clutched at the magic of new worlds to discover
Colour me in the turquoise of her winding path
Coursing under rainbows connecting valleys old and new
Trying to subdue the devil's rage that breathes inside my lungs
As the water flows over stones over stones
Alone in the fight to reach the sea
Alone in the shadow of the person I'm destined to be
Tenacious vines wrap around my heart and continuously squeeze love back into dreams
Climbing the backbone of the rolling hills
Standing where I blossomed, in a patch of spring
The radiant glow of sunset guiding me to a new day on the horizon
Calming the turbulence of a new beginning
My now awakened soul just moments away from living.

ROOTS

INSECURITY

Clouds roll heavy
Knotted and knitted into the grey
West to east an undecided flow
Trees bow, turn, lose their way and sway
Falling
Falling
Pressing ears to the earth
A landslide in the wake of the storm
Stand tall
Stand tall
Whispering oaks crown the shyness
Perturbation that quivers and grows
Seeds burst through to lightness
Rising
Rising
Towards the sky, quenching the tepid air
Filling leafy lungs, squeezing the void
Racing with the pulse of the rain
Bleeding sepia, leaving greens devoid
Monochrome mist bursts the calm
Beating
Beating
Bruising the skin
Curling the tattered edges
Translucent heartbeats as clouds roll in
She wins
She wins.

THE VOICE INSIDE

I am not good enough
I shouldn't believe
I deserve to love myself
I need to realise
There's nothing special about me
And never say that
I have the power to do anything
When I muster the strength to focus my mind
There's nothing good in me to find
When I see
I'm ugly inside and hate my body
When I look in the mirror I have no reason to believe
I'm beautiful
Then convince myself instead
I don't deserve to be happy
And the little lie I keep saying
I am never lonely
I've programmed myself to accept
No one cares about me
I'm naïve to think
I have friends and family who love me dearly
And not forget
People who judge me
To ignore
The real me I hide inside
I need to remember
When I have no reason to smile

(Now read from bottom to top)

WALKING SHOES

Days pass and merge like a butterfly from cocoon
A day too soon or late
My ambition waits on the verge of being forgotten
My footsteps march towards the silhouette in front
But I'm always drawn to the light behind me
Walking blindly but always kindly into the arms of my problems
I blame myself, my mind, my lack of self help
The thousands of dusty imaginations on my shelf
That I always promise I will read
Tomorrow and tomorrow and tomorrow
The owl calls for the third time
And I wait for the night to creep to sunrise
Page still blank but thoughts still full
I rise to the surprise of rain
And pull myself out of the same repeated morning blues
Into my walking shoes
And smile.

ROOTS

PEOPLE WATCHING

Under street lights and misty nights
Crisp leaves through winds that touch
Frost biting at weathered skins
On the people as they rush
I sit here through the mist of coffee
A warmth right to my soul
And watch strangers and new faces
And try to guess where they will go
It's the simple pleasures in life
Escaping in a moment, a sense of time forgot
Watching strangers through a window
Of my favourite coffee shop

SILVER DREAMS

As the mist settles it reveals a new world. Like fallen stars nestled in the creases of leaves, pools of silver dreams reflecting the autumn skies. The morning dew on the grass glistens and I listen to the rush of the stream nearby. Watching as the heron eyes the water with such stillness. I walk amongst the art of the woodland, fine angelic silk hangs between branches, surfing the light breeze as the huntress waits in the shadows. Vibrant earthly echoes of late blooms match the banquet of berries above, as golden leaves begin the autumn dance to the floor. I am anchored to this moment, awed by her beauty and the tranquillity with each step. In a magical world we only imagine, waves of pine and arboreal air. There in a place between day dreams and natures sigh. Breathe in the last breaths of summer and open your eyes.

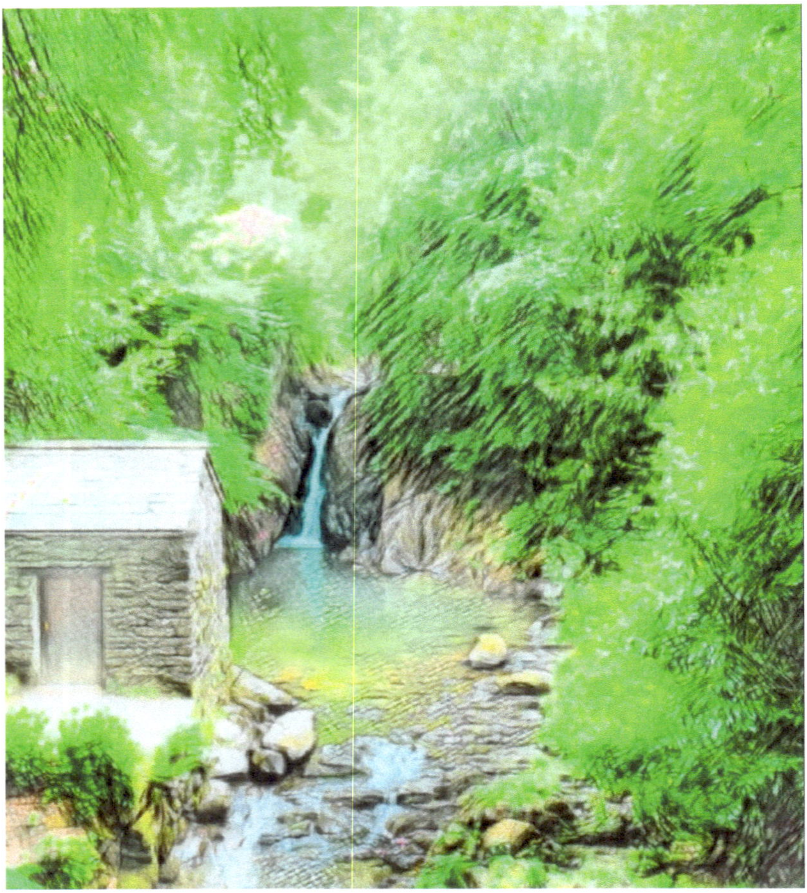

FLOW

There's something so eternal about watching the waterfall
A never ending flow
Like my thoughts that drip from my mind through my pen
A swirl of words that become crystal clear
In an infinity pool that never ends
The sound of white noise mixed with the hymn of the breeze
Alive with the limbs of the tree that praise the sky and welcome new rains
My pains disappear, soothed by the tranquillity of this irreversible river
I breathe in the sea green orbs that dazzle in the sunlight on ferns
As they envelope new pathways and swayed in the summary wind
The power of stillness with the roar of water that drums with my heartbeat
The white water weaves, flowing threads of nature's poetry
I am nothing in this endless cycle
An observer that sways through this short life
With the percussion of the trees and the chorus of birds
And the moments evaporate
They rise and create new clouds
Drifting along acres of blue until they burst.

AURA

Her aura was a universe that lapped the shores of her being. Mystic waves that weaved through a galaxy of star dreams. She was the sun by day, burning though time filled wishes and eternal reminiscence of darkness past. Storing a cosmos of her iridescent light to eclipse her soul inside. She was the moon by night, a crescent dream fading into the oblivion of new tomorrows.

HEART IN THE WOOD
(Inspired by Robert Burns)

I keep my mind in the mountains, my heart in the wood
No matter where I travel, it's here I'm understood

And its here in the country, where I stood, where I stand
My soul a rolling stone, carved from natures hands

I travel and I wander, chasing wild foxes and the deer
No matter when I return, my heart is never here

I keep my feet walking the highlands, in the direction rivers flow
No matter where I call home, it is the wild that I must go

I say farewell to my old soul, cutting roots straight from the ground
My heart is in the highlands, to the wild forever bound

I keep my mind in the mountains, my heart in the wood
No matter where I travel, it's here I'm understood.

SEA GLASS

There's beauty in the broken
Souls like weathered glass
Drifting on tides, sea's lullabies
Waiting on storms to pass
Rolling in lacey waves
Shaping a love formation
Dreaming in bodies of salt water
Magic of transformation
Born to seek out rays of sun
Whilst nestled in gritty sands
Tides smooth over sharpened edges
Unyielding shell built to withstand
Darkened storms of greys and blues
Sea mists rest on frosts of green
Weathered shards become a jewel
A treasure of the sea.

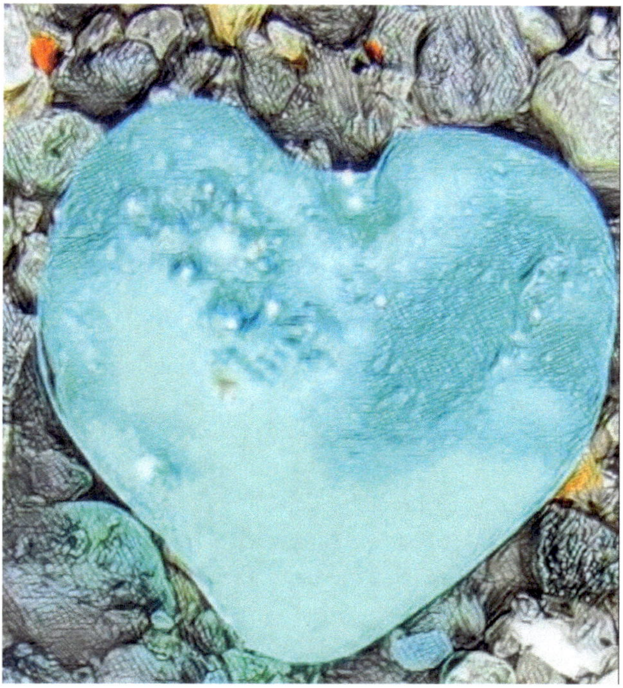

PHEONIX SKY

I sit in silent wonderment, breathing in the ruby painted air as enchantment sails the breeze. Sepia silhouettes of trees and whispering leaves almost hushed in the moment.

Red Velvet love laced clouds that leave a Tuscan glow on the ground, spreading gold in every direction. The poetry of the setting sun, the colour of hearts beating to start a new day.

The phoenix sky breathes fire into magenta dreams, weaving the northern light into the seems of my soul. A crimson curtain on days end, to send my wandering spirit into the unknown of tomorrow.

I close my eyes to the light to hear the dark as the sky begins to drain of colour and reveals a canvas of stars. Autumnal auroras kindle the sky in natures sway as the embers glow and the day fades away.

FORWARD

Acorns drop a marching beat to the path
Sunlight blinding the very view of the map
Burning soles shake the concrete hope
A now silent forest cut from rooted rope
Holding thoughts on winter's breath
Jump in lakes out of depth
Waves that rush the blood to flow
Rosey smiles and wilted glows
Underneath a seed bursts forth
Sapling dreams bloom from the earth
Between grass blades the magic dew
Emerald globes mask the subdued
Whispered words a reckless release
Blackened clouds wrung out with ease
Rippled reflection hides true form
Beautiful flower with petals torn
Moonlight glows over morning frost
Rolling pebble that never stops
Dreams the power of the shore
Wrapped in waves forever more.

EQUILIBRIUM

I wake, wrapped in my sleeping bag. The morning smell of fresh pines fill the air and I breathe in the sweet scent. A renewed sense of wonder fills my lungs and restores my equilibrium, light and dark once a battle for my heart and mind, to now find my balance.

To some I would seem lost out here in the wild, the only heart beating in this home is my own, but I've grown with every step forward. Wrapped in natures ever open arms.

To be outside is the only way to be inside this colourful world. To see each night magenta skies, followed by the twinkle of stars and a slice of moon for light.

I leave my heart in the home of another but my heart is left wild to wander. I've stitched my shadow into the ever changing tapestry of mother earth, oak tree and bird song together in one sensory palette that weaves my soul back into land.

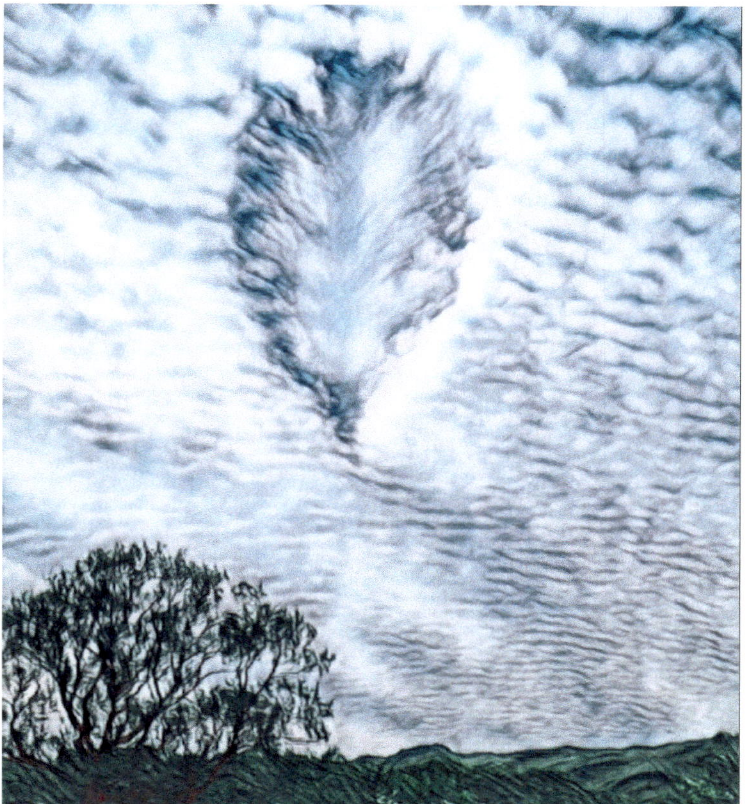

WORLD ON HOLD

I come in the peace of the wild things
Steady the heart with the birds that sing
Watching the sun wake through the grass
And the clouds roll as the time should pass
Silent mind and peaceful sighs
As the robins watch and the buzzard cries
Crossing bridges over gentle streams
A day spent in nature's day dream
And the rain falls and gently sings
Rolling on curves and dew dropped skin
Soothing the fire in my belly that lies in wait
Magic that the mind creates
Standing in mute silence under oak tree shade
Watching dusk burn the day to fade
Leaves laced with embers gold
Wandering to where the world's on hold.

DESTINY

I hold my future in my palm
As fragile as a moth under the crescent moon
Ready to fly in the calm of any direction
Dreams that lay in the hush of clouds
Wrapped in the winds of change
Until they fall like teardrop kisses to the ground
Stretching into the infinity of flowing rivers
Time cannot stop the flow of the stream
It shivers in the coldness of currents
Going around in circles finding an anchor
A revolution against the hold of anxiety
A cold war of an empathetic heart and the ingenuity of the mind
To find myself drifting through emotions
My soul as heavy as a stone that rolls and shapes with the storms
Ready to crumble at any fall
Stars only shine while the world sleeps
In darkness is where I burn the brightest
As shadows seep into my skin
Tattered wings that finally open and brave the elements
A fluctuation with the inhale of nature's breath
As the sediments of uncertainty settle within her resting heartbeat
The sunsets of tomorrow are never promised
The compel to fly towards its beautiful flame
A mesmerising unknown that will enrapture my soul
As the burning desire of dreams once again
Engulfs the path of my destiny.

CLEAR WATERS

Each wave stirred old memories
As the debris break and bleed onto the pebbled beach
My future becoming as clear as the waters
The mountains I seek in the distance, roll and stretch on the horizon
I breathe out the uncertainty from my chest
And let it rest and flow on the waters current
I watch as the swallows dip their wings and sing the chorus of new days ahead
The mystic winds to the unknown that lead countless dreams to this moment
A solitary soul in wonderment of seeking my purpose
Many enlightened feet have wandered these shores before me
As wordless thoughts become a vision of poetry
The calm pours over me as my inner spirit ripples on the surface and travels over depths of tranquillity
Time rolls away with the clouds and I close my eyes to the sound of the lapping water around my toes
I feel the rhythm of my wild heart slow in its quest for freedom
As my mind drifts and drips to write new chapters
And I watch as the water washes my words away…

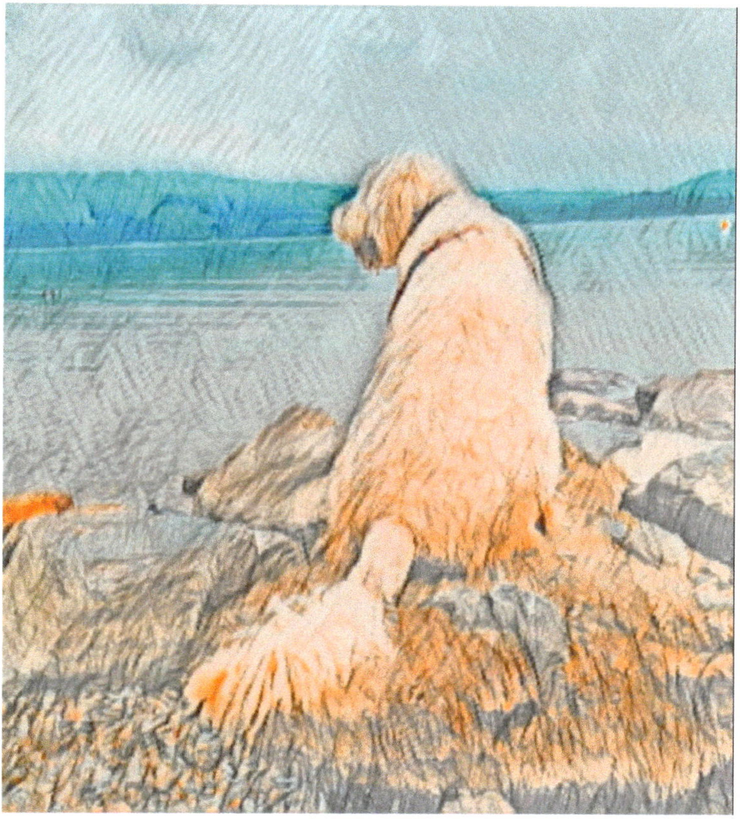

THE EDGE

I like being alone
Silence weights my shoulders like a blanket, warming the anxiety like a fire in my chest.
It's for the best though, to hide inside and avoid cracked pavements, cracked smiles, forced conversations and crowds.
To hear aloud the hum of these closing walls, suffocating condensed air that blocks my airways as I lie sideways watching the world from my window.
Sometimes though, I slip into my walking shoes and unstick the glue on these floorboards, passing the door and the hordes of other people in the street.
I get greeted with hellos, how are you? And smiles, holding open gates and they even share a bench with me a while.
I hate people though, yet they always seem to pull me out of myself, my hiding place amongst the shadows and the wedge I put between me and the world, avoiding the shameless temptation to fall off the edge of it.

PURPOSE

(INSPIRED BY WALT WHITMAN)

Oh me! Oh life! The question of purpose
Of the now, the worthless, the worry of endless
Of myself, caught between disbelief and the prayer
Of the footsteps of the great, we follow, we share
Of the eyes that see the souls renewed
Of the stepping stones we take to view
Of the air, the suffocating, surrounded in me
Of the solitude, the walk, the trees
Oh the answer, the now, the days momentous
Oh me! Oh life! This breath that was sent us.

DREAMSTRESS

I'm just a tailor made soul from mother natures sewing machine.
Freckled skin stitched to bone, I'm the dreamstress.
I've been the needle and the thread, stitching up hearts and having mine ripped in two.
I've sewn myself shut with only an embroidered smile. Dreams falling through the seams of my pockets, repaired with a patch of space and time.
My threads unravel for constant repair, while my steady fingers coax at the thread. The fibres of my being well worn and torn, disguised with pink ribbons and bows.
You weaved hope into my heart, patched up the blackened burn marks on the left side of my chest.
I became a figure redeemed by a replacement of seams. A pattern of us that ran parallel lines, interlocking ourselves as two combine. Stitched together by the needles of our pens. Binding the edges of my threadbare hem.
You ironed out my anxieties as my heart rate increases. Loved me enough to gather all my tattered pieces.
Unbuttoned my doubts and made love to my soul. A secure blanket wrapped around my all.

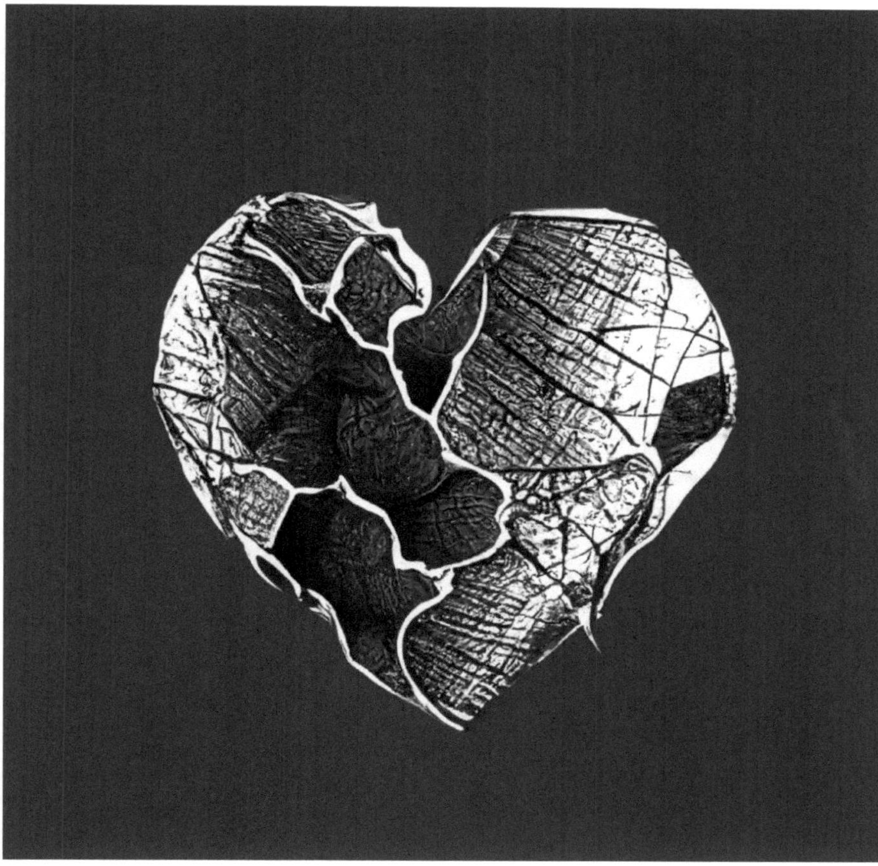

GHOST

I can say this aloud
Feel the breath in the full stops and watch the clouds steal my thoughts
As I'm caught in this place
Captured in the scenery
And the words chosen so carefully
The ghost of me left in the places I've been
But only I know the feeling
The drops felt from the ceiling as I fill my pockets full of rain
Smile always the same, hiding the corners of its reclining edges
The mountains were worth climbing
To leave a stone in a pile for the view
And descend back down with a soul renewed
A perfect picture in a frame
For a heart button wall of memory lane
But she haunts me
Taunts me and makes me feel empty
Like a shell that echoes the sea
Lulling me to a place of security
I meet her in the lonely hours
Follow my feet through the shadows
We are one and the same
You hide in the daylight, in the biting breeze on my bare neck
And the specks of dust that dazzle and dance in the fanciful beams of the setting sun
You might be the bravery that saves me
Adventure spreading like a disease
As you squeeze at the anxiety heart strings
Pumping adrenaline into my veins
I guess I can't live without you
No matter how many times I leave you behind
You are my true north
And the happiness will leave me one day
But you will always follow me to the grave.

PAINT AND POETRY

Time swirls the air
Wisping leaves into life
I now find you in my thoughts
Where you've been so many times before
Paint and poetry in clouds of memories
Conversations left and smiles you couldn't see
But it was all me
Turning down the duvet of winter's cover
Wondering why one is drawn to the other
Soft tones of your voice, warm like the sun
Winds of change we cannot outrun
She wraps us in the heathers of summers end
A chance, a heartbeat, given again
To walk within your company
Through the roses, the daisies and trees
I see you now
In the sunlight by the lake
Future dreams that we create
Letting them rest on the surface
But it was all me
Folding my arms because time forgot
The excuses I made for the time we lost
But still you hold me, wrapped in knots
Catching my breath and my heart to stop
I want to apologise
See you in every colour of the sky
Every shade of your eyes that give passage to your soul
To merge and radiate with my own
And find me in the overgrown wild
Untangle my feet from the vines
And let us sway in the breeze a while…

WRITTEN IN BLUE

It's the hardest thing to say goodbye
Choking the words behind tears
We cry
Loss leaves a deep hole in you like that
Not even the warming sun rays can reach the deepest pockets of my soul
Half of my moon missing amongst the stars
No one teaches you how to deal with grief
To deal with the pain that poisons underneath
Like thorned vines around my heart
Pulling and squeezing the hardest days we are apart
I long for deep sleep
To see you so brightly in the memories
Your laughter echoes in the flowers
In the bluebells, forget me nots
And I lay in them for hours
Blue all around me
In the river, the rain, the heavy clouded sky
I could paint you into the picture
Feel my breath catch as you smile in the sunlight
Fingertips tracing your silhouette
In fragmented visions and the trick of the eye
I could write you back to life
In stories, in poetry
In the words that you gave me
Blank pages of my vulnerability
An over turned inkwell, dripping from black to blue
Vividly loving you daily.

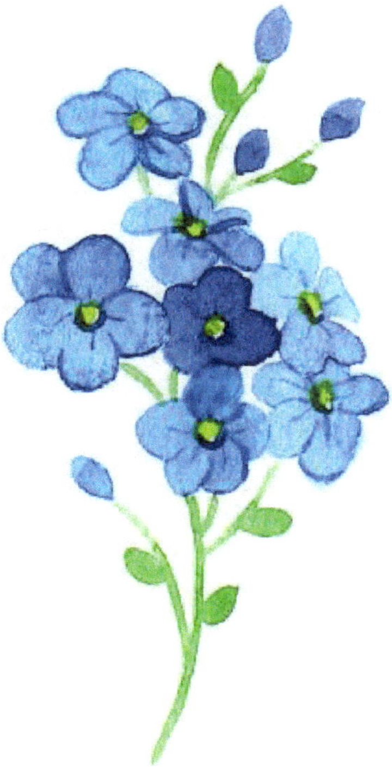

HOME

Take a deep breath
As you dive into the depths of my mind
Walk around into the shadowed corners
In the shackled dreams of the sublime
Enter the door to my kindness
And pour yourself a drink
As the whiskey burns to warm your heart
And scars it with my ink
Stroll across my corridors
Where my passion burns a fire
Sweat beads dripping down your skin
As you feel my loves desire
Tiptoe across the fragmented pavements
Fall into the black hole of my fears
Lie peaceful in the pool of solitude
Created by my tears
As the light hits the water
Cross the rainbow to my dreams
Where you will hear the echo of my laughter
And see a colour wheel of self esteem
Follow the distant roar of thunder
To my beating heart you roam
You will find your name upon the doorway
For within it, you will find home.

SKIN

Her skin is the cover to her book.
A soul wrapped in an earthen hue, worn out reflections and changing views.
Memoirs etched in the crevasses of crows feet, where past rivers have flowed and dried, becoming translucent with the contours of time.
Part of her wants to erase the lines, but the mirror tells her otherwise.
Each crack a chink in her armour, for even tough skin seeps pain in the veins to her heart.
Scars the tattoos of poetry.
Word riddled arms from the harms of youth, staring at this middle aged monster as it swallows her truth.
Hiding a soul that never aged a day, shining through her eyes embracing the change.
Wrinkles the maps of her incredible journey. Forehead tells the story of past and present worry.
Sun soaked freckles on weathered cheeks, paints the warrior that once was weak.
Fracture lines of emotions that trace a wistful smile at the corners of her lips. Luminous tones to her complexion that drank the light of the moons kiss.
A lifetime of shedding many skins, now accepting the ageing reflection of the body she lives within.

MAGIC

A sweet whisper on the wind
The magic of each breath I take towards your lips
Exhaling the words I love you
Inhaling each kiss I taste
As the wings of butterflies beat within us
Our love the definition of dreams
And through sunbeams and sunsets
Our love dazzled like the stars of the sky
Drifting like the ebbs and flows of a hurricane
We shook the earth that night.

ROOTS

UNREQUITED

And in that moment you smiled
It was like nothing else mattered in the world
I held my breath so that I could freeze time
Earth stood still but I was floating
Butterflies beating in time with my heart
In that moment I needed no stars or moons
Just you
And the sparkle in your beautiful eyes
You lit up the room and fire in me
A picture perfect polaroid in my mind I see
And it will stay with me forever
Brightening up my days of blue
Until the day you notice
I was smiling at you.

UNREACHABLE WINDS

I like to imagine my life in front of me, the gift to live and see a thousand moments roll in like thunder on the horizon of my heartbeat. I like to imagine you and me, walking along the beach, as we laugh and dig our toes into the sand. The fine grains of time slipping away with the tide and you smoke a cigarette to hide every worry.
Time drowns me, as unchangeable as the great loves before me and heading to a destiny that no one can predict.
I pull at every hope in my dreams, try to imagine your smile, a work of art that's stitched into the seams of my soul. I'm worried that I will forget you one day, life has a funny way of pulling you back to a reality of constantly trying to catch unreachable winds.

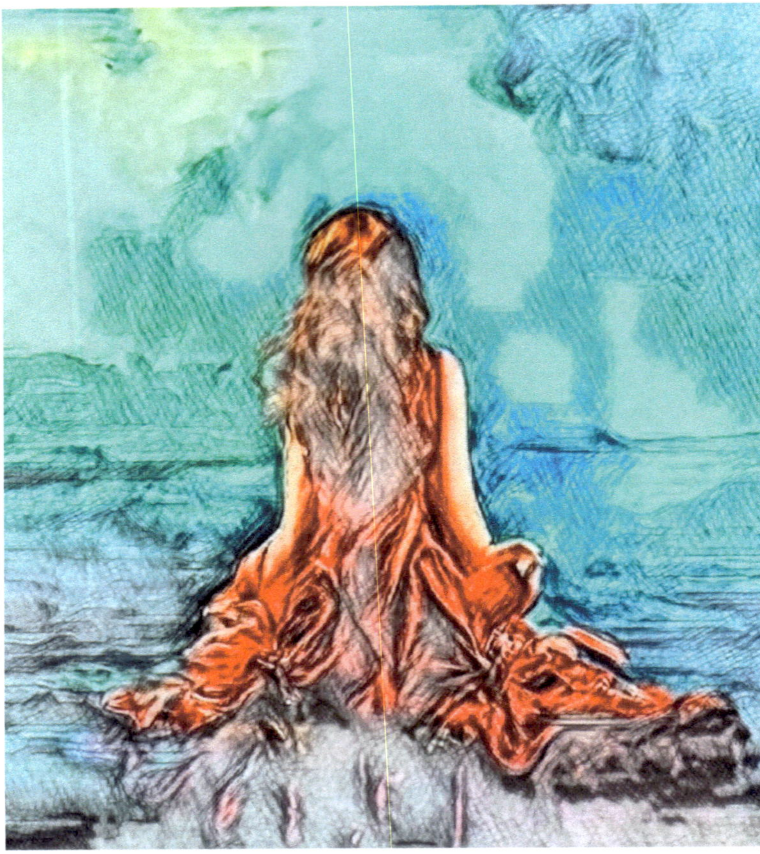

ANNABEL'S LULLABY
(INSPIRED BY EDGAR ALLAN POE)

I wish upon a star for you
Every waking day and sleepless night
You came to me in vivid dreams
My love, my one, my light

As they shine my fate, my path to you
Our love forever bound
My hand to hold in darkened times
The light of love was found

Twin fires that flicker through tests of time
Drawn through life like moth to flame
Our souls connected though worlds apart
The universe writes our names

I'm forever grateful for this gift of love
My lover of the sea
I gave my heart, my soul, my hand
Bound for eternity

Although they took my soul from me
The angels of the sea
I took my love, my breath, into the depths
Near the kingdom by the sea

Under night skies, my bright eyes
The stars that burn for thee
Moon that shines on the horizon line
As you sail the heavens to look for me

Through death we part, until the stars
Align a fate to see
My dreams, my path, my destiny
Will bring you back to me

And so here I lay, by the ocean waves
In my tomb by the sounding sea
And I will remain your love, your one
Your beautiful Annabel Lee.

NEVER OUR TIME

Missing you comes in waves
A million saves, a million ways
But still a million miles apart
I've moved on, moved home
Moved mountains since you've been gone
But still my compass points towards you
The end of a rainbow that fades with time
With the memory and the words
That was yours and mine
Left in a place beyond our control
As another summer rolls by
I don't know why
I think of you when the birds sing
When the night time silence clings to my skin
When the words of rescue roll like thunder
And I'm under our memories spell
I hope that you are happy
There's a reason why leaves decay
And new springs shoots of change unfold with the days
Love blows with the wind
Words will never fade
And with time we carry on
But the what ifs and maybes
Are never truly gone
I hope that you find love
Even more special than yours and mine
Met once through destiny
But never quite our time.

DREAMSCAPE

What's it like through your eyes
To see me the way you do
And express me with such poetic lies
Words so beautifully written
They suck me into a dreamscape of imagery
And suddenly it's about you, your romantic disposition

But you aren't like that are you?
You are an artist, a Wordsworth, a visionary
Using words to capture the minds of few
You burn out your loneliness with whiskey
Maybe it strikes a fire in your heart
And inspires you to write what it sees

But you will never know the real me
The person behind my own witty over used lines
No, you will only see the girl with the smile
The girl in which you use your words to define
It's clever isn't it, how you construe
The poems that touch your mind and heart
And make you think they are all about you.

LOVE TO DREAM

I can always remember the way you smiled at me
Those wild eyes and the way your cheeks dimpled
The way my heart glowed
And the night sky twinkled like fireflies
I can always remember the way the grass felt under my bare feet
The way the rain felt upon our skin
As I stood on my tiptoes to kiss you
The way your lips tasted of the night air
I felt like I was floating on a cloud
Lost in the music of nature
As we swayed in my dreams.

LONGING

What do you say to a soul
So lost in wild
Rattling the winds
Through ribs and spine
To cry in woodland pines is a lonely silence
And leave all what was then behind
Sun blushes the heart
For a second to feel the warmth
And the dawn of fresh lips on skin
Bones on bones
And the mourning of light in the eyes
What do you say to a soul longing
Tethered to the stars
And the radiant moon
Swooning in the dreams of absent touch
Relentless in the persistence of need
Like a vibration of bees to a flower
What do you say to a soul craving
Forgetful embrace
As leaves kiss the collarbone
A scent of sea salt and musk
Embedded to the ground
Stone on stone
In the breath of earth
Slowly turning to dust.

I NEEDED YOU

I needed you
Like the stars need the light of the moon
You were my sparkle
The tide that brought me to shore
When I'm lost in waves
In my mind once more

I needed you
But you were the white noise of the rain
The thunder in my heartbeat
As it tried to escape my chest again
You were my sunlight that dries up rivers on my cheeks
You were my legs, my strength
When my knees felt weak

I needed you
My whisper in the breeze
Gently brushing my skin
Making my soul at ease
You gave me the air in my lungs
Love in my chest
Light in my heart
Putting my worries to rest

I needed you
But you left me alone
With my thoughts, my darkness
Not even a call

I needed you
Left in pools of memories I lay
Each night fighting dreams
As each day you fade away.

YOUR SILENCE

Was it just the words you gave me that I loved
How they reached inside me
Touching the tips of my soul
Or how they inspired me to spill my own inner workings
Onto a page for the world to see

As the ink smudges and runs with my tears
In your silence I am lost
My inner fire I cannot kill
You had a heart so full yet a mind so distant
You took my very breath,
Yet I long for you still…

EARTHS EMBRACE

The wind combs through my hair
Weaving and pulling as it whispers its breath into my ear
I hear the call of thunder as the clouds grow heavy with want
A need for release as it teases drops of icy kisses on my skin
Thirsty for the rains sensual wonder
I keep walking, climbing over the roots of nature's feverish veins
And brush through the wild it contains
A fleeting euphoria, surrendering all that I am
Under the ancient serenity of trees
The melancholy of autumn sinks its teeth into my flesh
Tasting the last honey dews of summer as it catches my breath
I have no resistance as I'm wrapped in the embrace of her existence
A seductive victory of the seasons
As my senses peak as sweet as cherries that burst on the tongue
Undone as the day slips away under the grip of night
A volcanic passion that burns deep as silhouettes dance under the moonlight
A smouldering heat of bones that entwine together
Rising with the roots from the ground
Inhaling her exhale becoming one
As the morning sunlight waits to cradle me in its arms.

TEACH ME HOW TO DANCE

I want you to teach me how to dance
Tap dance along dreams and seamless fantasies
Let me do a ballet on my toes to kiss you
Spin me around into a dizzy haze of contemporary love just to crave you
Let your tongue waltz to the hum of craving lips
A feeling of bliss
As my legs wrap around your body like a hot tango
Your love like liquid adrenaline straight into my bloodstream
Our bodies screaming as we move in freestyle
Fast and slow
Losing breath
Bodies locking
Twisting, turning
Yearning for one more dance
Let us romance
Let the music rock us back and forth
Whispering lyrics into each other's ears
Your skin like cashmere
I want to glide to every place on your dance floor
Twirl my tongue to taste your soul rhythm
Move with every ebb and flow of your love notes
Let us float along the sweet vibration of our love
A bolero of twin flames, burning desires and lust
Thrusting us into a sensual rumba
Grab my hips and sway me into a paso doble of orgasmic ecstasy
A fantasy
Of you and me
So tell me
Will you teach me how to dance?

KISS ME

Kiss me beneath the willows
Under a waterfall of leaves
Kiss me where the sunlight touches
As our fingertips are weaved
Kiss me as the blossoms kiss
The pastels on a breeze
Kiss me as the rainfall touches
The horizon of the sea
Kiss me in secret
Wrapped in your ivy vines
Kiss me under buttermilk moons
That stand the test of time
Kiss me as the river flows
As I drown in your diamonds blue
Kiss me with natures promise
Where my future lies with you.

BITTERSWEET

He didn't quite believe in the fate of the stars
I was always looking up
Hoping our names would be written in that black inky space
While he swirled sugar in his coffee
A dark sweet pleasure of thoughts on his mind
I guess it takes two views to see the depths of love

Bittersweet.

WATER AND FIRE

I walk your shores
Memories crashing around my ankles
Alone in my mind once more
Soft edges frothed like champagne
And once again I'm drinking you in
The same thought
The smiles we caught
Now trapped in this reflection
Where the heron bows its head
And the breeze curls around my spine
You are mine
Lost in time and borrowed sunsets
Raindrops fall and create a river dance to your rhyming rhythm
And I sit warm in your silver mist on the bank
As beads of kisses nestle on my skin
A kingfisher threads the surface
Vibrant tones through the dusk of night
A call to my darkness
You are my light
As the moon nestles among the oak leaves
Heaving heart beats through the roots of our tree
You are the love of my life
And I will always find you where the water weaves the clouds.

ROOTS

JEALOUSY

Shining green in the eyes of the beholder
Born in love and produced by fear
Crying out in tears of anguish
A glimmer of cupidity in desirous eyes appear
Manipulating with foul tongue
On a pursuit of personal gain
A creative spark of envious lies ignites
Like green gasoline on an unrequited flame
A circle of loves devalued trust
Through emerald sight
A treasure of lust
A heart that yearns through fires smoulder
Blue and yellow haze of the days of love lost
Shining green in the eyes of the beholder.

SPRINGS ROMANCE

Oak screen canopies
Hides the silence among the trees
Heart beats to pulp but the sap wont seep
Dreaming of a vision I long for you to see
Lies split leaves and crunch defeat
Limbs on limbs wrapped in complete
Butterflies in the hollow flap their wings
Floral subjects of delicate things
Blowing dandelion wishes in the mist
Rains dry up where the sun has kissed
Sycamore seeds dance with delight
Above the clouds and out of sight
Blind flutters of wings under the moon advance
To streams that whisper spring's romance.

STUNG

Melody of fluttering wings fill the air
Iridescent rainbows of your love affairs
Floral existence brought to life by you
An army of love makers
The flower, the fool
Pollinate with your words
Your soft hum of fantasies
Misleading sting vibrates their soul
Blossoms dancing on daydreams and fallacies
Coloured hues of pink
Tarnished with yellow stained promises
Sweet nectar turned to sour
Drinking from the garden of the goddesses
Making honey from their essence
Tasting beauty as petals part
Feeding the craving
Never loyal to one heart
They bow to the sun and cry with the rain
Whilst you take pieces of their soul
Until they wilt and fade
Forever prisoner to the earth's constraints
Broken in the darkness
Until they rise with spring again.

ROOTS

WAVES

Memories of yesterday and promises of days to come
As the storm rattles an emptiness in my chest calling for home
We walk her shores through the sea spray of airborne lace
Tides tied around our ankles in a whisper of waves
Anchoring our emotions, inhaling love in our lungs
Swaying on the percussion of her steady pulse
We redefine treasure as I placed my heart in your hand
Sharing a divine space, creating silhouettes in the sand
Fingers running through hair like wind swept dunes
Perfume of salty sea on skin, gazing into your eyes of ocean blue
The horizon our future, through sunsets and sunrise
Building dreams of forever with you by my side
And when distance separates the sea from the shore
We count the moons until our souls are together once more.

BURN THE BOATS

Burning the last heart strings that tied my ankles to the hurt.

Burning the insecurities to put me first.

Burning what's left of the memories inside.

Lighting a match to burn the bridge of you and I.

Burning the bricks and a year of walls that I built.

Watching flames grow devouring the guilt.

Burn the last pieces of my scorched and scared soul.

Let the embers drift and make me once again whole.

Ignite my future, my island and rekindle all dreams of love

Burning the boats to a new life for us.

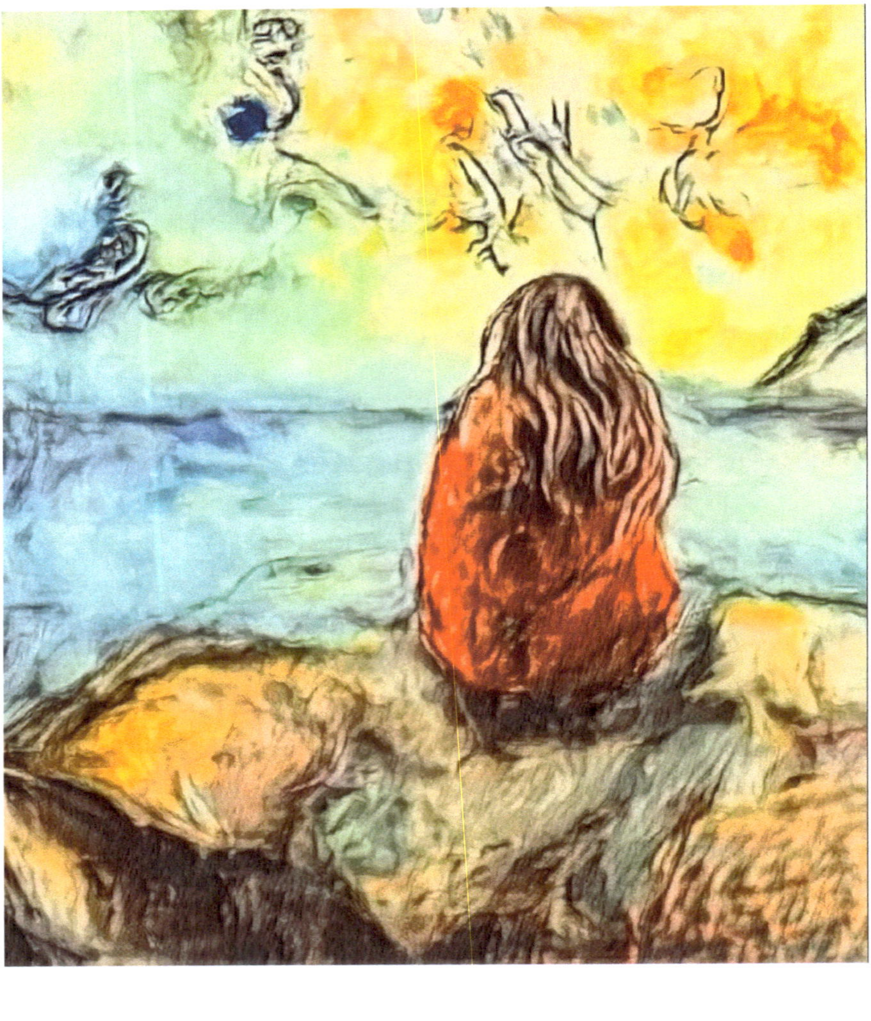

LETTING GO

Why is it all the good things I remember about you?
I can't go anywhere without this nostalgic bliss
My toes curl into the sand where I stand
Sinking like the feeling in the pit of my stomach
As I remember why I had to leave
I grieve for you like you are no longer on this earth
You faded away with the bruises you left on my arms
But I stand here now feeling the sea spray on my lips
Losing my breath as I remember your kiss
Why do I miss you?
The wind whips my cheek, a pain too familiar, leaving a cold residue of tears
Not because I feared you, but because I loved you
I could never say no to you
I was just a vessel, as empty as this shell in my hand
Your hateful words echoing through me
Roaring like the storms of the ocean
My devotion to you hurt me deeply
Yet I remain, like a sandcastle waiting to crumble beneath your waves
Adapting and reshaping to suit your weathered moods
Soothed only by your warmth, a break of sun in your dark clouds
Until I was finally allowed to love myself
I grew the courage and the wings of the gulls
I gave myself a bird's-eye view of the real you
And I knew that by letting you go
I could mend this deep abyss of a hole you left in my heart
I stare at the horizon now, where the clouds meet the sea
Where my distant memories remain of you
Now at peace within me.

SOUL OF EVERYTHING

Your laughter is the soul of everything
A contagious burst that makes my heart sing
Laughing at the silliest things
And we can't stop
The fragmented air that leaves our lungs
And strung a thousand moments in our memories
Like stars writing our destiny
Lighting up the darkest days
Lifting us spellbound in the sweet music of happiness
And I cannot suppress the love I feel
I'm addicted to the sound and the feeling it brings
Your laughter is the soul of everything.

SWEET NOTHINGS

I imagine waking up with you
Sun dancing on our skin
The way you smile at me
Drawing me into your lips
Tracing lines with my fingertips
I imagine you holding me
Whispers on your breath
In my ear, my heart, kissing my neck
As I let myself drown in you
I imagine us so deep in love
Undulating waves wrapped around your soul
Swimming in sweet nothings
Every morning you're home.

DEFINITION OF LOVE

I'm intoxicated by you
Captive to the beams of your heart and soul
Ancient roads lead me back to your being
You are my Rome, my home
Like soft crushed velvet, reflective of light
This love I have for you
Takes me higher than heights
A sacrifice
There's nothing I wouldn't give to bring daydreams alive
Not written in words, yet emotion
Not heard in your voice, but your eyes
And I lie in your arms, bathed in your warmth
My purpose is to love
My purpose is your soul
Our love like a candle immune to the winds
Blowing over oceans, connecting two flames
You are the sky and the clouds
Gentle rivers and bird song
You are the air that I breathe
In my heart you belong
You are the ether of magic
Moon dust from above
You call me an angel
But you are the definition of love.

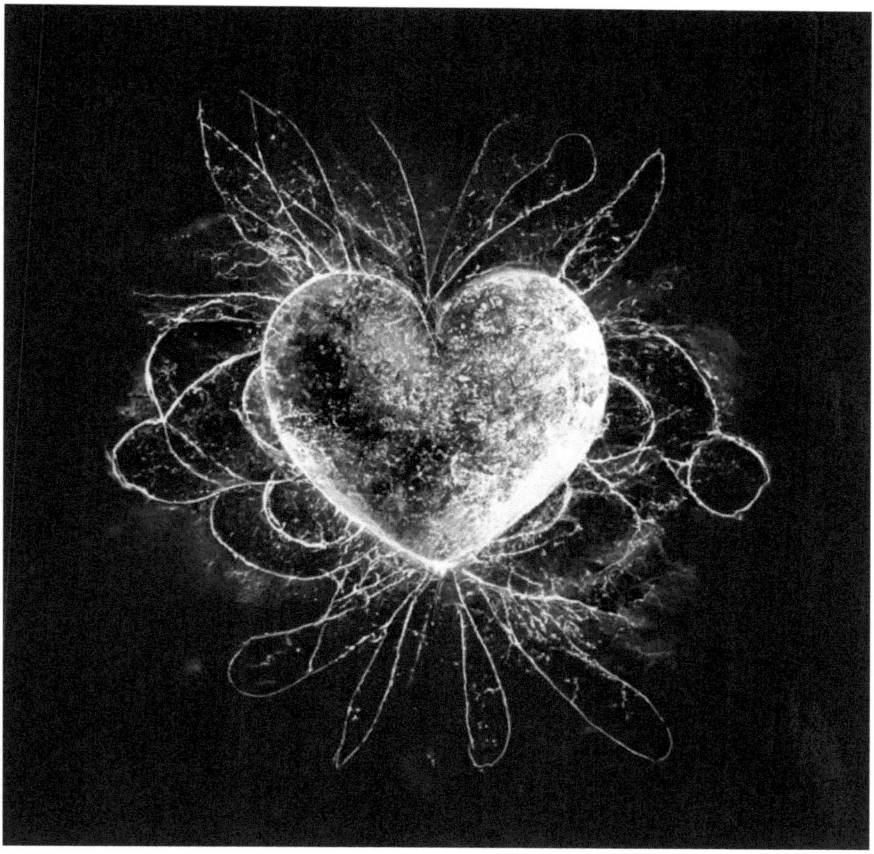

LOST IN A MOMENT

As the flowers fell from the moon
Like an ovation for the love it looks upon
I crumble at your feet
Like soft pink petals under your fingertips
I'm moonshine in your eyes
But a mere sparkle from the stars as it hits the ocean
I wanted time to stop
As the world disappeared under the spell of your kiss
There is no talk of destiny, aligned stars or fate
But we found love in this night
Lost in a moment.

MY LAST LETTER

You opened up my heart dictionary
Emotionally naked words beating to life
I whispered them into the night air
To let them find you in your darkness
A deafening silence broken by love
You rescued my soul in your pages
Like bird song in the dawn light
I lie fate in the palm of your hand
Burn quietly waiting
A flame forever yours
In the letters you wrote
I love you…..

Je pense toujours à toi

STARS

But what of the stars
Little seeds of dreams
Planted in the seams of the earth
What do they know of love?
Of loss, of souls that die
Little lights forever
In skies of emeralds, blacks and grey
What do the stars know of the moon?
Of you in the darkness
In tune with the trees
And the autumn leaves
As they twinkle star dust on frosted ground
What do they know of silence?
The sound of your heart beat on mine
And the limited time
Of your hand in mine
Oh what do the stars know of eternity?
Of the safe place above the sea
A prison of scintillating love with no key
Do you think they will reserve a place for you and me?

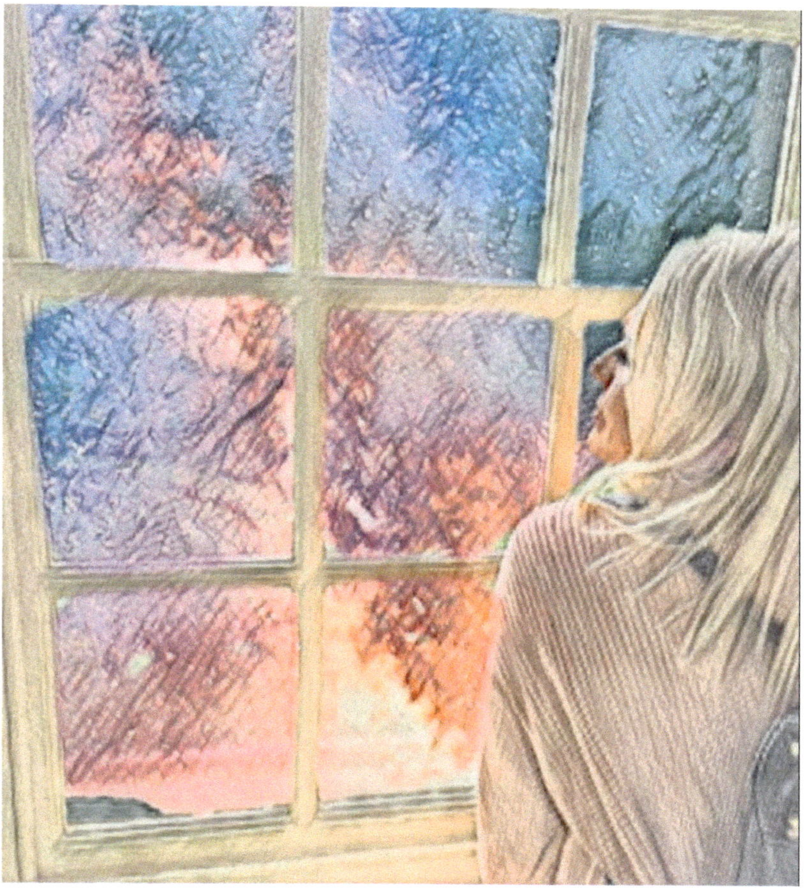

YOU ARE POETRY

You say you aren't a poet, but to me you are poetry

You are the key that unlocked my heart and soul, the magic wrapped around my all, as you trace the constellation of freckles on my skin.

You are the wordplay that tickles my senses and leaves me hungry for the alphabet I taste on your tongue, coming undone as it travels on an endless sensual landscape. Shaking the earth like lightening, I am stunned awake in a safe place between your heart and the stars.

I am awed by your presence, a moment of quiescence as the world around me slows and you write poems that create goosebumps on my heartbeat and leave me in a myriad of emotions.

You say you aren't a poet but you lasso my soul with your pen and adhere your words to my bones. You are the marrow that fills the voids of my broken pieces and traces the creases of my smile with pixilated ink.

Together entangled in rhyme, dancing on the rhythm of words. Fairytales in fingered pages, turning chapters and floating on a cloud of ever afters.

You say you aren't a poet, but you are poetry to me.

ROOTS

GEORGE

Here...
In this moment right now
Not thinking about a future, not licking the wounds of my past
Or even reminiscing the good parts
Barking mad up the wrong trees
It's just me and my dog walking in the rain
Soothing the chest pains and anxieties
He looks at me like I am the only person on this earth
Follows me like a constant shadow
For I am his light, his guidance, his protector
A connector of two souls in a short lifetime
I sometimes wish I could live like him
Running free of worries, running free from emotions
Commitments, dreams, money
They say it's a dog's life but I never really knew the meaning until now
I mistook the beauty of it
Maybe we could learn something from it
Live life day by day, same routine
Sleep, eat, repeat and play
No working our fingers to the bones, no concept of time
Just always here
In this moment right now
I watch him play with other dogs
Constant chasing with no intentions
Not chasing for connections or to be liked
Not chasing for compliments or answers to life
Not even chasing for love
Just the pure enjoyment of feeling the breeze

These are the days we should remember
Sitting by the cold lake wrapped up in December
I'm thinking about my life, constantly chasing my tail
Thinking when will it begin
And I look at him, looking at the murky water and back at me
Silently asking "Can I jump in?"
I smile as you raise your paw in my hand
Tilting your head to try and understand
Waiting for a command with true love and devotion
I get emotional to think how lucky I am that you saved me
Forever in your debt and helping me see
All the wonderments of this world and all that surrounds me
Here
In this moment right now.

BEAUTIFUL LIFE

I've drowned what felt like a thousand times
In water, in love, in the big decisions in my life
I've ridden the fear but been afraid
Every
Single
Time
I've stood at the top of a volcano and mountain peaks
The ebbs and flows of what we seek to fulfil in dreams
I forgive easily, I've loved hard, followed blindly with broken hearts
I've seen marriages and births, the suns eclipse
I've danced on shore lines, in the rain I've kissed
I've written my own stories, turning pages of words and poetry
Learnt that my imagination is a place they don't see
And I've burnt the bridges and letters to realise time doesn't make it any better
Just to forget you
I stopped chasing the corners of dead end streets
For fear of purpose and what might be
And see that today is enough
I've fought the good fight, lost friends, gained more
Crossed paths, opened doors, battled anxiety, won the war
Adoring the lungs that allow me to breathe
And feel lucky at the things I see
With my roots, my family, my tree
My truth in times I don't believe
But I stand proud in myself, in my skin, in my shoes
And see what a beautiful life I've stumbled into.

Printed in Poland
by Amazon Fulfillment
Poland Sp. z o.o., Wrocław